Crossroads
of Change

Poetry & Messages

Cheryl Lunar Wind
and Friends

Crossroads of Change

Poetry & Messages

Some of the poems in this collection first appeared in Come To Mount Shasta, Star Messages and May Love Lead chapbooks; Fractal Reflections II and on facebook.

Cover photo credit to Jeanie Bridges, 2024

First edition.

Published by Alexander Agency Books,
Mount Shasta, California 96067

ISBN 979-8-9897287-9-4

Crossroads of Change

Poetry & Messages

Crossroads by James William Kaler
(reprinted with permission)

We are now at a profound crossroads, where the veil of illusion, once impenetrable and seemingly eternal, has been unraveled. Those who built and defended the Illusion feel the ground shifting beneath them, and, whether they admit it or not, they sense that the sands of time are slipping away from them. Their arsenal of deception—the tried-and-true tricks they've used to keep humanity bound in shadows—is now empty, exposed for what it is: an antiquated mirage, hollow and incapable of holding sway over awakened minds. Their rhetoric, once potent in its ability to divide, to instill fear, and to create obedient followers, has dissipated like dust in the wind, and they stand defenseless, their hold on reality vanishing.

We are witnessing the dawn of a long-awaited balancing—a moment when the natural laws of cause and effect are in full swing. All that was misaligned, manipulated, or used to hold people down is now coming into alignment as a greater truth emerges. This shift is not merely a passing trend but the very real and necessary adjustment that was bound to follow the centuries of imbalance, exploitation, and secrecy. We are part of a universal rhythm that is self-correcting, and this is the time for that correction, for the restoration of balance. The chains of illusion are falling away, and those who see through it can feel the liberation and energy of this new era.

This time is nothing short of a gift. It's a profound opportunity for those of us who have seen through the Illusion to step fully into our light and purpose. We salute all those brave souls who have stood steadfast, who have pierced the darkness and brought awareness to others. Through their courage, the illusion was not only revealed but understood, which has brought us all to this moment. To see past the façade requires strength, resilience, and trust, and now we all stand as witnesses to the end of an era, a testament to the power of truth over deceit.

And as we move forward, let us remember the wisdom of the ancient martial art of Aikido, which teaches us to let negative energy pass by without resistance or opposition. We do not need to fight against the Illusion or those still defending it; we only need to let it fade away. Like a shadow chased away by the morning sun, it loses power in the face of the light we hold. We do not need to engage, argue, or convince.

There is no need to exhaust ourselves against the remnants of what is already crumbling.

Instead, let us save our light, our energy, for building the world we want to see—a world rooted in truth, unity, and purpose. Let us focus on the creation of a future untainted by the distortions of the past, and allow the remnants of the illusion to pass, knowing that it no longer has a place in our world. Those who stand in awareness do not need to defend their knowing, for truth speaks for itself. In silence, in steadfastness, we have done what was needed.

So, we move forward, steady and unshaken, letting the old energies dissolve as we give our light to what will truly endure. Salute to all those who have seen, to all those who have dared to speak, to all those who have held the torch. We are stronger for having walked this path together, and now we stand on the threshold of a new reality.

"Oh Divine and Everlasting Spirit,
We pray that Your Mighty Power
May fall upon the World---NOW.
We pray that this might enter all men,
So that they may have some small
Glimpse---even though but dimly seen---
Might be forever a monument at the
Crossroads of their inspiration."
---*The Twelve Blessings,*
The Master Jesus

Preface

In the fall of 2024, when the tail of comet Atlas broke off
energies came in on the sun's rays--
Like a pinata at a children's party, showering gifts & goodies;
bringing back to Earth ancient majik--
Gifts, in the form of past life memories and abilities.

Here in this volume some of us from the Mount Shasta area are
sharing the precious downloads received from this cosmic gift.

"Shifting currents
in the psyche of Awareness

bring to Zero point
the fulcrum of change
where Silence speaks Wisdom.

Tread softly to listen deeply."---Mercy Talley

"The most sacred transitional operation is ongoing beloved--
Once again, analyzing and judging the actions and decisions
of others is only going to create confusion--

We say again, this is not about them and what "they are doing"...

This is about you.

God."---Le'Vell Zimmerman

Contents

Sovereignty
by Cheryl Lunar Wind

There is a call--
eternal and subtle--
Step into Sovereignty.

Join the Ball,
Melodies are Ringing,
Singing, Bringing--

the ancient dance
it's in the blood--
You can not ignore it.

Each will go there,
sleep walking
compelled, like a trance
we are led--

The Divine Calling...
was always part of the plan.

The alarm clock has sounded--
the Sovereign Awakening.

Words are Homeless, Words are Home
by Kazi Ayaz Mahesar

Words are not just weapons, words are prisons as well. Words sing of freedom, words are caged in cave. Words are living, words sigh and breathe. Words see and are seen, light years in their eye, moment in their voice.

Words are voice, words are voiceless, words are vision, words are blind. Words are just, words are cruel. Words stir their lips, words make them cry. Wise and not wise, fool and not fool. Words walk, walk away from voice. Words talk in silence, talk in grace.

Words are naked, words are clothed. Words are thorn, words are rose. Words are sling, words are nuke. Words are shot, words are blast. Words are dust, words are mist. Words are earth, words are sky.

Each cloud a conversation, each rain a negotiation.

Words are leaders, words are cheaters. Words are peace, words are war. Words are vigilant, words are carefree. Words are rapprochement, words are estrangement. Words when they are words, words when they are chaos. Words when they are rumbling, words when they are sweet. Words are winter tales, words are bitter almonds. Words are Iced pomegranates, words are melted chocolates.

Words are woods, words are cleavers. Words go protect, words go chop. Words are paper, words are boats. Words migrate, words go borderless. Words are secure, words are vulnerable. Words are lighthouse, words are hurricane.

Words are ships, words are piers. Words are ocean, words are ports. Words are that they trade, words are that they strike. Words are that they connect, words are that they disconnect. Words are that they open, words are that they block. Words are that they sing, words are that they dance.

Words are wonder, a wonderland, a hot balloon, a spacecraft. Words are Moon, words are Venus. Words are one great leap, words are one great fall. Words are villages, words are first cities, words are towns, words are silk routes. Words are highways, words are bandits. Words are pundits, words are doomsayers.

No doom until they utter, no bloom until they say. No reason until they reason, no season until they wish.

Words are summer, words are spring. Words are cherry trees, words are autumn leaves. Words are dandelion, words are wasps. Words are dawn, words are chameleons. Words are snakes, words are charmers. Words are magic, words are apples. Words are adams, words are eves. Words are sighs, words are sleeves.

Words are light, words are dark. Words are peace, words are war. Words are drones, words are thrones. Words that they fly, words that they trick. Words that they crawl, words that they kill. Words that they die, words that they live.

Words are tombs, words are wombs. Words are evil, words are nurse. Words are prophets, words are prayers.

Words are echo, words are big bang. Words are first creation, words are last created. Words are gods, words are angels. Words are fairies, words are prairies. Words are witches, words are riches. Words are priests, words are prisons. Words are wood, words are fire. Words are decree, words are pyre.

Words are disease, words are cure. Words are lepers, words are helpers. Words are anger, words are kind. Words are music, words are dance. Words are rivers, words are seas. Words are world, words are Heaven. Words are thrill, words are throne. Words are hopeless, words are hope.

Words are Homeless, words are Home

This Day
by Cheryl

The morning is full of expectation--
the cold white sky behind
the very still pine needles,
one brave pine cone
looking at me.

Glimpses.

peach yellow light
Far
in the background.

Each
holding their own hope,
secrets to discover
this day.

Grandmother Pine by Cheryl

So much gratitude
for sunlight on
long, an elder tree--
like the deer who
carries a large rack
on his head.

The sky and tree branches
combine in a kaleidoscope
fashion-- small shapes
of blue peeking thru.

The huge pinecones represent new life.

The Frost
by Dustin Wood

We grew up together - you just never noticed me...

I tried to get your attention. Weekly.

Daily.
Sometimes even hourly, but you just looked right through me.
Like I was a ghost. A reflection of something you felt you could
never be.

Sometimes you would say or do something that made me think you
knew me. I always felt the coldness attached to the lack of your
acceptance but then, suddenly there would be a sliver of light.

I would chase it down and try to transform myself to become the
size of that sliver, so I could just live in that light forever. But as
quickly as the light appeared, you would snuff it out and patch the
hole it came from.

That was always the worst. The coldness always feels worse after
you get a sip of the warmth.

Sometimes it takes everything inside me to not scream in your face
"I'm right here! Just acknowledge me!! Just a glance or a nod so you
know I exist! If you do that then I can help you!"

Instead, I just sit in the frost that builds up on me. Hard to tell
where the bitter cold starts, and I begin.

One day it's going to become too cold. One day I'll be snuffed out
by the freeze.

What a curse my existence is. The power to change lives but no
voice to speak it into existence.

If i could speak I would say just one thing:
We grew up together - you just never noticed me...

I am your confidence.

5

November 3
by Janet Demeter

November winds sweep through the narrow mountain town
Its little streets and eager trees alive with the promise of dawn
The rich, dark skies prepare for the sun's rise
With wind chimes tinkling and dancing their joy
Of a new day's awakening to the Mountain's delight...
Still sleeping minds are at ease with no lingering thoughts of the schemes-

Brought from the winds of yesterday, as the river laughs
And flows along its perfect, winding path
Full with the nights share of light of the Milky Way
Carrying love, inspiration and hope of the Universe
To the river's southward realm of sprawling and gargantuan reach,
The Gift of Mother Earth...

11:11
by Cheryl

Did you know that numbers and colors are codes?
Ask the crow--he will tell you.

November.
11:11 is the code for awakening.
A great flood of light is upon us--
We are at the threshold.
White light streams
from father Sun to mother Earth.

We will all become as children--
delighted, playful, innocent

It's your birthday!!
"The former things have passed away."

In the new higher dimension--
I hear the singing, ringing of the words--
om mani padme hum

It is the Universal Chant.

I have the feeling, We've been here before.
Avalon, Arcata and Deja vu

An Invitation to Receive
by Shivrael

Children laugh so hard
and are so happy!
It's as if it is your birthday.
They are so pleased

that
you are you,
and that you decided to incarnate
fully as human
So you could be their mother, father
sister or brother.
We are all in this together.

Let's be playful.
Wear bright colors
expressing a higher octave
of emotional expression.
Let's cross the threshold
of pure delight,
better than we have
ever experienced.

Collectively humanity
will cross the threshold
this November
to higher octaves of joy.
The gifts to humanity
are coming soon.

Open your arms.
Open your heart
and fully receive.
Codes drop in packets
from the sun.
My heart interprets the truth
from this highest timeline.

A message within
reminds me
to stay in my highest joy

and greatest peace
while passing through
the portal to the other side.

Take That First Step
by Le'Vell Zimmerman

Once you begin to step forward, the path will appear.
If you don't begin to step(take the chance),
you will not see what's next.
Trust is required to begin.
You will only know what you need to know,
when you need to know it.
Masters know peace...
This is why Masters know all.
We have no questions.

#3333

At the Crossroads of Change
by Shivrael

When change comes your way,
that you were not expecting,
you land at a turning point.
Something is ending
that you counted on to be there.
Your sense of stability is rooted in.
The world as you know it now
is shaken by the news.

You felt the Tower moment was coming
Now change is upon you.
The foundation of your life
feels like it is crumbling,
but it is really transforming.

You are a butterfly.
Embrace change as metamorphosis
so that you can fly.
Even if you can't spread your wings yet,
trust the unfolding.
You are bright and beautiful.

In that moment when you feel lost,
summon the Guardian of the Crossroads
to remind you of infinite possibilities,
and that this turning point is a gift
that allows you to shift
your life to a new timeline,
to a new playing field.
You can be or do anything, sister.
"Infinite versions of you are possible.
So claim them!"
says the Guardian of the Crossroads
(also known as your higher self.)

Feel the freedom and liberation
in change.
Ride the wave,
Surf the light
into the safe shore of your own being.

The lighthouse is you,
Your grounding and security.
It is not anything outside of you.
As you shine your light,
you illuminate the path ahead-
every step of the way,
into your transformation.

You are leveling up.
Enter new hallways of experience fearlessly,
knowing that you are safe.
Your home is in the heart,
and Source guides and supports you
opening you to the field of infinite possibilities,
also known as miracles
which are your divine right.

Tower
by Cody Ray Richardson

What has held you back is a great source of power.
Under the tower. Over the tower. Beyond the tower.
There you are with a butterfly on a string.
Crossing the abyss yet again.
Oh what treasures will you find?
What will you give away?
What will you keep?
Everything we have we must loose.
The only way not to loose it is to give it away.
There you have it. This one is for you!

Eagle's Transmission
from Sabina and Herd of Light

When the ego-sea of humanity
and each
individual ego-drop within
fully Sees that its True Nature
longs to be of service
to something,
and fully Sees its confusion as to who it is truly in service to...

When the ego Sees itself
as servant to the expanded Self,
as the servant of the Sea,
not of the drop,
But to the drop
within the Sea who Sees
the Sea within the drop...

Then,
this True Seeing
of True Service
liberates Flow
between ego and True Nature,
unfurling wings of True HUmility
and of True Majesty
in One
    fell
       swoop.

~ With All our Love, Sabina and Herd of Light.

Crossing Bridges
by Shamballa

I cross the bridge,
over and over, and still
I need to cross it again.
Seems this journey
goes on and on--
We reach a plateau
or a point where we
think we have arrived, and suddenly
all over again--
We must strive, strain & struggle.

Feeling lost,
searching for maps
grabbing at phantoms,
seems to be the fool's destiny
I partake of greatly,
Reaching for phantoms, thinking they
will satisfy-
my thirst
my hunger
my heart

And once again
I start to cross over the bridge.
The stream is beautiful, especially
on a morning like today--
with the sunlight reflection
on our way.

Bridges by Mercy Talley

Bridges to new destinations
suspend over transitional chasms . .
when crossing, let go of being tethered from where you leave,
view where you venture to
instead of looking down,
Be Present With Breath
for companionship
keep walking beyond the edge
into the heart of Nature's embrace

13

Eternal Song
by A'Marie B. Thomas-Brown

When there are no words, the silence speaks
When there is no joy, the sorrow leaks
When there is fear, courage arrives
When truth is present, it erases lies
When dusk is falling, the nightingale sings
When Death tolls, the bell rings
When all seems lost, hope appears
Where desire abounds, temptation is near
From the ashes of Remembrance, we hear the song
That only mothers can sing, and brings the prodigals home
Lips of vision, tongues of grace
Lift my heart higher, as new seasons we face
Carry us on, to new heights and deeper depths
Moment by moment, breath to breath
We arise from the ashes, to sing our new song
Love lifts us up, where we belong
A wave of the hand, crashing against time
We all hear the sound, with ears to the ground
Thumping a beat, that silences doubt
One with our Source, unending Peace abounds
Raptures of sovereignty, authentically One
One body and mind, one moon and one sun
Galaxy drifters, Omniverse in full view
For the kingdom, indeed, resides within you
With every sunrise, new mercies I see

A Turning Point of Grace
by Shivrael

I went to bed with
I love life.
I love life seduced me
and I started having more fun.
I forgot to worry so much.
I started slowing down
inside myself
so that I landed in the moment.
I love life showed me
that being here now
was enough,
and is all there is.
The present moment
is the turning point of grace.
I am sliding into Now
more easily than ever
since I took I love life
into my bed.

I'm mixing I love life
into the water that I drink
I'm letting it in and living it,
drinking it down so that
I love life combines
with the essence of my being,
and I become I love life too.

To stay or go
by Cody Ray Richardson

To stay or go
Does it really matter which one I choose
Am I the orchestra
Am I the orchestrator
Knowing the meaning of the orchestration is more important
than who is in charge
A game
Real change
Who is to know
Uncomfortable means it's real
Will I uphold my past way
Can I be molded into someone new
Realization came through pain
A glimpse into someone I strive to be
It's easy to repeat
Nothing wrong with easy
Time to break the loop though
This fantastic journey
What a masterpiece I am
I see myself through you
Thankful you have shaken my pattern
No matter what happens
I am forever changed

Go go go!
by Mikasa Tamara Blue Ray

Christ Consciousness Portal of Unity.
Take chances and embrace the unknown
Your happy path will be shown
Explore new possibilities
Myriads of abundance symphonies
Enthusiastic
Fantastic
An invitation
To your happy destination
You never know
What awaits you, so Go go go!
Through this Portal
You are Divine, Eternal and Immortal

Deja Vu
by Cody Ray Richardson

The moment that I see her face
Deja vu hits like a eerie reminder
Everywhere I have been
The future, the past where I am now
Tossed about in different realities
Bigger forces throwing us around
I am a thirsty plant waiting on the shore line
She is the sea
Oh you wicked moon
The ebb and flow you cause
Gives and takes her away from me
Can I pull up my roots
Break away from what I'm attached to
Walk to stable land where I may wither if I do
Will the tide come and wash me away as I wish
Forever drown in the ocean of you

Sea of Compassion
by Mercy Talley

Healing so strong
broken hearts
dissolve in the wave
of potent Love
becoming
The Sea of Compassion
washing the muddy rivers clean . .

Souls Lifted Up
in the Brilliance of
Everlasting Truth
Of Love's Depth
Great Mother Father's
Arms to receive All Home Again
~~~

From my Heart to Yours ~
Hawkwomyn soaring
on wings of Hope
in the midst
of it all

Soul-life Currency
by Maria Louisa

The Soul-life is the currency ~
  So let go
    and let Love Be.
      The Soul-life is the currency ~
  Surrender
    and be Free.
      The Soul-life is the currency ~
  Be Still and know that
        Love Holds Thee.

The Return of the Dragon Mother Oracles
by Elaine Marie Rose

These feminine oracles were once the sacred living spirits that wove the umbilical cord between the heavens and the earth.

They resided in the temples of living light that held the resonance of the purest imprints of Creation.

Their role was to bring through the plasma flow of energy that became the wisdom to sustain the civilization they were guardian over.

These living temples were arrayed across the planetary grid and hummed with the harmony of biogenesis creation. They were energetic waystations that imprinted the divine blueprint of peace, abundance and health.

This healing network was the binding point from which life as a civilization unfurled around it.

The Grail Kings and Magi knew of the paramount need to provide this sacred space for the Mother's and as master builders created and sustained the infrastructure of the Dragon Priestess Temples. These were living spirit temples, alive in all ways.

This network of support to the Divine Feminine Oracular Wisdom later translated to the King's Rite Initiations, where the Grail King would, by his ritual union with the High Priestess as the vessel for the Goddess, be blessed in his rulership of the lands and endowed with Divine Authority.

These ancient archetypes are being restored and coming to life beyond mythical fairy tales and ancient stories. These patterns of life have existed upon the Earth throughout time, in eras come and gone and long forgotten in the mists of fragmented minds and hearts.

As the descent of divine power was usurped into the false hands of tyrants and thugs the feminine oracles were eradicated and their energy enslaved, and the lands fell into poverty, ignorance and desolation.

As the covenants are fulfilled these ancient rites of the true Divine Sovereign Template of Sacred Union are returning.

As the Mother Dragon Christos Queens and Solar Father Christos Grail Kings remember, so shall it become our way once more.

Where are the Ancient Temple Builders? The Master Architects that built the inexplicable power of the towering glorious cathedrals of light and frequency we find as mere remnants and relics of their former glory and splendor?

You are being called to rise again.

Remember why you came here.

Arthur's Seat
by Rune Darling

THE GALACTIC COUNSEL OF 13
Has been Assembled at Arthur's Seat
The Meeting is Adjourned
.

We Pledge to Vote
Only from Our Open
White Heart Burning in
Pure Passion of Truthfulness
.

Decided it is
To Rearrange
The Runic Alphabet

So ᛒ & ᛗ Will Up & Out
In Togetherness For Eternity
.

Gaia & I sit at the Round Table
We know what to do
We know Our mission
.

We pledge to all there is that
We won't rest until it is fulfilled
Our destiny
.

What Is Up Must
Now Come Down
.

Don't Choose Side
In Any Conflict
Us and them is the Illusion
.

Choose Love
Above All
.

Evil And Good
Right And Wrong
We Shall overcome
.

A rainbow bridge flows inside us
Aligning the chakras is the key

Liberation is at hand
Once again we shall be free

.

Heart-Mind coherence leads us to
The Holy Grail and
Cosmic freedom

.

At Iona in Orans Chapel
Excalibur revealed the frequency
To Untie the Gothic Knot

.

Now it's up to all of us
To walk the talk and sing the old songs

.

Star Sisters and Brothers
United we must be to see
What is right in front of us

.

Dunsmuir is Avalon
by Cheryl

Calling all knights--
and virgins alike.

Come to Avalon-

We will meet at the Round Table
where equality and leadership
Reign Free. Sovereignty.

Rub elbows with Merlin, Guinevere and Morgan La Fey--

Join the ancient dance.

Pierce the veil...see through the shards

Cloak and dagger--
Knights and swords-

See through the shards...

Morgan La Fey's ghost
whispers to me...

Dunsmuir is Avalon.

Prophecy Uncloaked
by Bonnie Bailey

The virgin parts her veil
sacrificing the alchemy of her yoni
uncloaking the prophecy.

A storm of ghosts
of the patriarchy
at the round table
dissolving her equality,
leadership and centuries of wisdom.

The spirits of Huachuma
piece together the shards
of the feminine kaleidoscope,
the ancient dare of empowered wisdom.

The Mushrooms, Merlin, Mystical
Mycelium invite you to your
authentic self.

Lay down your sword and
take up your staff.

Standing in my Sovereignty
by Jennifer H.

Writing in a dream,
phantoms of my true authentic self
watching me from shards of broken glass-

The promised Avalon waiting for me,
All eyes on me, will I fulfill the prophesy?

What am I willing to sacrifice
when knights of darkness come at me
with sword and staff, will I bend, or break.

What am I willing to allow them to take?
Nothing!

Standing in my Sovereignty.

Dancing the ancient Dance of Power
letting them know they can't keep me
locked in their tower.

Guinevere, Merlin & Morgan La Fey
all hold council.

Watching the storm unfold
as I alchemize, the facade dies.

The Broken Mirror
by Jennifer H.

The world's sadness in a storm,
seeing far and forlorn
Distance, the world's biggest illusion
Everybody standing in one place, all
occupying the same space, it all
taking place--at the same pace
yet we pretend to be disconnected
all shoveling the same lie, it's not me
I don't have to see you,
Ignoring the missing piece, standing
there in front of you, breathing within you,
crying out, reaching, seething,
grasping for care, for air,
till you want to rip out your hair
Staring in the Broken Mirror
not wanting to be broken
Ignoring the missing piece,
I don't have to see you.

Angles
by Cody Ray Richardson

Though the reflection is not as clear
Now your view has been shattered
Look closer not away my dear
There are more angles to view
In a broken mirror

Round Table
by Shamballa

Merlin whispered "Come to the Round Table"
his leadership evident in his presence as we sat.

Suddenly our eyes opened and Avalon was all around us; a sense of
equality was present in the very air and sovereignty was inherently
evident.

A pillar of alchemical light suffused the tower, the Ladies and Lords
were in equal measure around the Round Table.

Merlin guided them with soft subtle gestures into a profound
communion meditation each feeling the miraculous Wonder of
Oneness and the angle of their unique authentic collaboration in
bringing the prophecy into fulfillment.

Age of Chivalry
by Cheryl

There is a calling-
to come home-
Home to our true self.

Leaving behind- any veils... patriarchy, matriarchy.
Alchemizing, Returning
To a self-led monarchy-
where all are the leaders and the servants,
equivocally.

Stepping thru the kaleidoscope-
fun house of mirrors

Emerging past the shards, angles and phantoms--
We become the Merlins and Guineveres of yesterlore,
drinking mushroom laced cacao and Huachuma.

We are knighted.

The ancient dance storms in our blood.

In the tower moment, we drop our cloaks--
Remembering we are the virgins to sacrifice,
ghosts to haunt and fairies to play.

Prophesy prevails.

The Age of Chivalry
has returned.

Karmic Kaleidoscope
by Kazi Ayaz Mahesar

How is it like sleeping in cell
How is it like walking in hell

How hot the buckets full of water
How bitter the taste of the cactus

How long this labour of lost days
How long these pangs of the night

How can any creator, of any genre
Create so fragile, or so like rocks

What's in the silk you're weaving
What's in the stone you're carrying

Sweet oil? Of raisins and olives
Of the gardens of Lamporecchio

From Florence, Vinci where it is
ANCHIANO, to Leonardo's place

Where muse makes his Mona Lisa
Where prairies become his paper

Where he knows no high no low
Where he moulds his clay dough

Sharpened eyes iron blade in hand
Bleeding heart spongy rain in sand

Whence the world sinks and sails
Whence the winds know no wails

Where firs slumber in their sleep
Where dragons glow in their deep

Whence the wild gets wilder
Whence the mild gets milder

Sixty thousand years of solitude
A day a dawn, a night a ride

A day in dungeon fiery dark
Karma karma, a keyless lock

Kalos eidos scope, ghel n green
Clear crystal now as it has been

No high no low no up no below
All harvest a plough, as we sow

Dirt dirt, dirty harrys
Blue purple all the berries

Tear tear veils of the dark
Clear clear, lights at last

Hearken to the Raven's Call
by Aria Squire

In the dawn times arose the blue raven tribe
calling out the message for the listening ones
To gather round to share the sensing, feeling, knowing
that are rumbling and rolling like thunder
in the cavernous depths of the souls abode
Irradiated by lightening bolts of luminous perception
speaking truth into these Now times
Hearken to our winged message
born of the velvet void of creation
Fear not the unfolding mystery
of wondrous fresh becomings
Embrace the spectacle and power of our beneficent sun
as it flushes, flashes and flares its fiery golden rays
onto our precious earth and body temples
Heating ones blood, bones and passions
Igniting the hearts fervour and awakened spirits to rise
Remembering you too have wings upon which to fly
Beyond the density of mind clouded
with both confusion and despair
Seeking desperately outside the moment and outside of self
for answers that lie within
hidden in plain sight
Obscured by attachments to former realities
steeped in foolish notions of control
making one impervious to what can be shown
and in eventide truly known
Unshutter your sacred eyes
Unfetter your heart
Allow your soul to truly guide
revealing the shining path that beckons you onward
Descending and ascending on a spiraling journey
to discover the source of the virgin light dawning
Beyond the shrouded veils, views and news
that clamor for your precious attention
Recall that where attention goes
energy f l o w s
Deep dive into crystalline rivers
Fluidly flowing into streams of consciousness
where you can ride pristine currents of knowing
Allowing the ancient ones, your star kin
to gently nudge your soul freedom bound

Where you may rest peacefully
within the azure eyes of the coming storm
Secure in the promise of purification
that will reign down upon
the firmaments of old
opening new earth upon which to roam
Washing clean the wounds that over time
have festered with bitterness
led by the false sight of hate
Armed only with compassion
the blisters of rage shall be lanced
For they have grown in the shade of ignorance
unaware of the need for humbling light
that is capable of witnessing with love
all that remains unseen
Hidden judgments of self and other
snares and traps of the egoic mind
lost in division and illusory separation
Begging with muted cries
for the anointment of true forgiveness
given and received
as One
and the same
Allowing for the return of unified consciousness
to work in tandem
to birth co-creations
of new ways
new days
and new earth rising
Where the collective knowing is evolving
and so chooses to willingly and intently
live, share and be in embodied presence
Awake to the miraculous
inexhaustible
power of love
abundantly seeded in all
Greet with honour the life bringers
bearing water for the verdant tendrils of life
innocently sprouting forth
Root deep with felt gratitude
for all that is freely given
to sustain all life
Reach then for higher ground
beyond former imaginings

Upon which to grow anew
the brilliance and splendor
of creations beauty divine
Celebrate the glorious
return and resurgence
of light encoded beings
Infused with compassion's grace
within which only love
can truly gift
and humbly abide
An awakening golden age is on the rise...

Clearing of the Mists
by Shivrael

A prophecy has declared that
the veil is now lifted.
Revealing seven sisters in cloaks,
across the water,
The Isle of Avalon is now in view.
Their alchemy transmutes
and calls the power
of the One Creator of all
To bring humanity to the
round table of Oneness.
All beings sit as equals
no matter their age
or station in life.

An ancient dance, remembrance
brings the coalescence
of hearts mended and united
for the redemption of the people
and the salvation of the children,
offering safety and protection
for every being.

He who went first is now last.
She who was left behind, is now ahead.
The meek shall inherit the New Earth
because the heart's frequency
wins the day.

And we shall play,
in the co-creation of the
New Paradigm that
we've waited for forever,
now here on Avalon,
spreading like wildfire
across this holy planet
In every holy moment,
bringing us closer to who we are
and who we came here to be as a people.

Gods, Goddesses and Gurus:
The Holy Quest to Unfuck Thyself
by Rene Moraida

Life on this planet can be exhausting.
In my insomnia I scroll through the gram, seeing beautiful pictures
of people having a good time, in Peru, Hawaii, and other spiritual
tourist destinations on our holy Makah. While I toss and turn under
the sister light of Grandmother moon, I yearn for belonging, desire
a partner, and check my banking account to see if there's enough
dollars and cents for a veggie burger tomorrow, much less a
vacation to escape my reality and wounded separation.

The spiritual quest to unfuck yourself and create a new script is also
exhausting.

The numerous options to choose a god, goddess, or guru are like
dangling golden chains in a pawn shop.
Shall I sing mantras to Krishna and Kali or wander the banks of
Mama Ganga for a sadhu to become my guru?
Or do I join a coven and play with my fellow witches, casting spells
and binding those who need to be bound.
Do I surrender to Yeshua and become a Christ, or pray to Mika'il
and the angelic realm?
Is my answer at a well in Glastonbury or in the arms of Ama?
Will my peace finally come at the feet of Avalokiteshvara or in the
halls of Valhalla?

These golden threads call and beckon:
Buy me! Get another for half off!
No thanks, just looking I say, shutting the door on transformation.

This shadow work they speak of, "doing the work", is equally
exhausting. While the heart yearns to be fearless and open, the ego
mind spews venom and negative feedback loops, the darkness
blocking out the sun rays of light.

Where is the manual book on being human? So much to heal and so
much noise, it's really this not that, you should take this, not that.
Introvert, hypersensitive, anxious attachment, anxiety, occasional
depression, needs a rescuer, fragile, approach with caution, handle
with care.

Who would come close to this wounded animal? Does the stench of regret seep off the corpse of this brother who does not feel fully alive? Not enough rose oil and nag champa to cover up his journey through the hell realms.

And yet, amid the exhaustion, the desire to love these broken and wounded pieces remains. The holy quest to unfuck thyself is a path upon itself, a dangling jewel at a crossroads to heal or...continue to suffer.

With every song to Shiva or dance with a kola in the forest meadow, with every spoonful of honey, and each mindful sip of tea, and every hour slept, and every step walked on a sacred site, and every flower gazed upon, and every tear shed, and every poem written, every prayer spoken, and every candle lit and spell cast, every chakra balanced, every massage received, and every kind word uttered to self--all this--is holy work in creating a new script, a new chapter, a new beginning, a new life.

THE EMERALD CITY
by Cheryl Lunar Wind

Lahaina is Lemuria
And
Mount Shasta is Atlantis

the jealousy and back stabbing that existed
in those ancient times is prevalent today.

Are we doomed to repeat history?

Those who think Mt. Shasta is the emerald city--
Beware of pitfalls.
There are witches and wizards along the way,
who only want to trick, mislead and see you fall.

Rotten bananas.

In the fruit salad of life,
there are more than a few bad apples.

Whole civilizations have collapsed---
Burnt--Gone down in history.

We are at the same Precipice.

Lot pleaded with the Lord if there were at least
10 good men/women left...would they be enough
to stay the fires of Heaven?

How many pillars of salt on the horizon?

It only took one person consumed with jealousy
to sink Lemuria and her inhabitants.
In Atlantis, it was a group of scientists, the Elite
who considered themselves above the law.

How many humans are like that today?

They say they want togetherness and love--
but their guest list is limited.

'Invite Only'

I'm pretty sure my work here is coming to a close,

And it is with sorrow that I say I have great concern
for the human race.

There is a catastrophic failure in the catalytic converter---
the place where emotions are transmuted, cleaned and cleared.

Those of pure heart are seeking asylum.
I thought this was a safe place.
What's the saying? It's a nice place to visit
but I wouldn't want to live there.

The inhabitants of Telos keep safe by locked gates.
We are not allowed there. We can visit in our dreams;
but when we wake up, it's back to the same.
Adama says they are rooting for us.
And--
if I want to join a zoom call for $29.95
I can talk to him.
No thanks.

Some lessons from Lemuria and Atlantis:
_We are in a new day/dawn which calls for the dropping of old
patterns and ways. We need to learn new ways of doing and being.
Another important lesson is to open our hearts in compassion and
forgiveness. We must purge ourselves completely letting go
of any pain and anger stored up inside. By doing this we heal the
core wounds of humanity._
---The Legend of Altazar by the Hermit of the Crystal Mountain

Life - An Art of Transformative Living ...La Vie En Rose
by Mikasa Tamara Blue Ray

In this dance of existence, let us Rejoice
For life is a canvas, and we are it's Voice
Life can be a Canvas, white and Unknown
With every heartbeat, a brushstroke of its Own
The wandering Heart, oh, how it Beats
Through laughter and tears, each challenge it Completes
An art of transformation, a delicate Dance
No guarantees, just chance after Chance
Decisions unravel like threads of a Seam
Obstacles defeated, transformation Extreme
Here in this temple, the body we Know
Senses ignited, emotions in Flow
Thoughts in circulation, swirl and Ignite
Sometimes the ego of judgment, emerge from the Night
Away with the fears, out with the Doubt
Welcome the now, let the past fade Out
The present embraced, constant love in the Heart
A tapestry woven with courage is an Art
Human encounters, awaken the Soul
Each loving response, a piece to make Whole
Life, the transformer, liberation's Key
Years of existence, a symphony played Free
To love, to work, to dare and to Dream
To dance through the storms and let your spirit Beam
The outside world rages, purging the Fight
Yet within there's a silence, the truth shines so Bright
Curiosity blooms, trust fills the Air
Gratitude wraps us in joy beyond Compare
Life, the contemplater, whispers so Sweet
The magic of living, in self-love we are Complete
A surprising journey, a masterpiece Spun
In every shade, our stories are Won
So, embrace every challenge, let the heart Sing
Together, as One, we create what love Brings
Dreams unfolding, happiness Anew
Life, transformed: an art, bright and True
La vie en Rose: Blooming roses sway, in the Heart's gentle Space
Opening petals in the SUN's soft Embrace
Joy dances in colors, so vibrant, so True
Positive thoughts bloom in rainbow Hue

High vibrations hum, like a lullaby Sweet
Unity beckons, where all hearts can Meet
"Remember," they whisper, "we're not far Apart"
Each soul united in a note in love's symphonic Art
Look, it's aligning, on canvas, in life's Rhyme
In the now, we're shining, we're shifting through Time
So hold on to love, let your heart softly Sigh
For in La Vie En Rose, together we Fly
In this dance of existence, let us Rejoice
For life is a canvas, and we are it's Voice

Loving Frequency
by Shianna Freeman

Frozen waters
Earth daughter
Mountain high
Rainbow bright
Blue sky
Crystal eyes
Tall trees
Slight breeze
Raven song
River strong
Eternal flow
Eye know
Time slows
Earth glows
Leaves descend
Many ends
Here's to death
Cosmic breath
Star dust
Self trust
Nature lovE
Dirt rub
Free feeling
True healing
LOVING FREQUENCY

The Great Return Home
by Cheryl

Round Table
Threshold- Hold on.

Super Sun & Super Moon--
Hold on
We about to fly--
Heating up-
Head to toe--

Light
all around,
I feel love.
Looovvvee

Deliverance
by Rune Darling

THE RAINBOW WARRIORS
WILL BRING HOPE OR
DELIVERANCE THE 13
OR DECEMBER

.

In My Human Form
I Walk Through The Night
Delivering Love From
The Heavens Of Lights

.

I Am not Afraid of The Dark
Because Here On Earth
I Met With Angels From The Realm Above

.

I Call Upon Them Once Again
To Tear Down These Walls Of Men
Lucifer Bring Venus Our MorningStar

.

In This Dimensional Layer
Real The Darkness is
The Balance is Off
Nations Cry Out War

.

Sisters & Brothers From The Stars
Blow The Trumpets Now
Let The Idea of Nations Shatter
Truth & Love Shall Now Be Our Matter

.

Evolve Like The Butterfly We Can Too.
The Human Race Must Choose
The Path of Light or Darkness

.

The Medicine Wheel Spins
Out of Time To Fulfill Our Spiritual Destiny of
A Golden Age : A New Era of Consciousness

.
Healing Fast We Are
Now, Here, in The Now

Accept All There is
Speak The Cosmic Tongue
.
Fear is The Frequency Mace Humanity Now Will Face
What YOU Choose to See
Becomes YOUR Reality
.
With Nothing But Love
In Our Open White Heart
.
Enur Darling

Eye Am
by Vivian Marie McIntosh

A Master Builder
By Human Design
Called Manifestor

Down To The Core
Truly A Hermit Fool
Enigmatic Jester

Third Eye Open
Three Fold Flame
Heart Initiated

A Threat To The
Darkness And Demons
They Get Agitated

Surrounded By Evil
That Can Not Dim
This Internal Light

Faithful Warrior
Of The One God
Shining So bright

Avatar State Activated
Accessing Abilities
Of ALL Past Lives

Awakened DNA
No Longer Dormant
It's Ancient And Wise

Resilient Roots
That Touch Hell
And Able To Bend

Planted In Sacred Ground
Blissfully Growing
From Heaven Sent

With A Life Mission
Of Manifesting
A Whole New Earth

A Golden Age
New Renaissance Era
Humanity's Rebirth

We go empty
by Pradeep Nawarathna

Naked you come,
Naked you'll leave.
Weak at the start,
Weak at the end.
No money today,
No money tomorrow.
First bath by others,
Last bath by others.
Why hate?
Why fight?
We go empty.

Inner Beauty
by Pradeep Nawarathna

Your mind shapes your face so bright,
Inner beauty shows pure light.
What you think will soon appear,
Reflecting who you are, sincere.
The heart's true landscape starts within,
Where beauty's journey will begin.
Look deep inside your inner space,
And see the beauty of your face.

Ouroboros
by Danielle Divinity

I finally understand the plight of Sisyphus rolling the boulder
up the hill, Being human is to accept that the work is never done,
There is always another void to fill,
And yet, there is nothing new under this burning sun.

What happens after enlightenment?
"They" say you still have to chop wood and carry water
But I was expecting a change in environment,
Life feels to me like an abandoned house feels to a squatter...
If I can see with real eyes all that was once lies,
If the external is a reflection of the internal
Why does suffering still litter the skies,
And why do we still burn here in the infernal?

Change your perspective,
Choose to see the light in the darkness of night
Says the spiritual collective
But as good as the imagination may be,
you still need actual wings to take flight.
It's clear most of humanity still lives in fright.
Humans don't understand they are cannibals regardless of their diet
We are the ouroboros eating its own tail,
We are the screaming in the eternal quiet
We are God experiencing what it is to be frail.
We are cutting ourselves open to feel alive
We are demons masquerading as angels
We are glitches in the hard drive
We are forever dressing ourselves in labels
And still no closer to figuring out who we really are
So we continue to treat life like a costume party
Each of us wanting the spotlight but forgetting we are each
composed from the elements of a star
Each of us so fragile but pretending to be hardy.

I can't help but ask, "but what more is there?"
I am the child who always asks too many questions
I am the one who stares God in the face like a dare
I am the one to whom the devil whispers confessions
And I refuse to die until God gives me directions.
-DMB is We

HU-- You Truly Are
from Sabina and Herd of Light

Re-uniting your glance of attention Light
Here and Now,
with the non-matter
of your Being,
the non-matter That Is
HU You Truly Are,
re-turns you to Coherence,
your natural state
of ease.
This frequency of Essence Light,
is the non-matter of each appearance as matter.
No matter what seems to matter,
you are non matter at your core.
And this non matter of
HU you are
matters.
It is the non matter of you that allows you to shine
no matter what seems to matter.
Your shining, matters
and re-matters All.
With Love,
Sabina and Herd of Light

Matter by Cody Ray Richardson

Thought proceeds matter
Your matter is forming around us
For us
By us
We care
Be careful
Be full
Care
Rainbow bright
Your bright
Light
Frequency

"Time and space and matter are malleable, add to that the fact that all life and matter is connected by a web of intelligence, logic and life drive--all of a sudden miracles if you will are just common place."---*Darrel Johannes*

Tree Talk
by Janet Demeter

Subtle, quiet, but very real is the speech
Of the tall and lovely star beings,
Majestic Masters who tower over us all
Offering healing as love and peace to those
Who would sit, and wonder, and gaze
In awe of their beingness,
Quieting the mind for the soul to hear.
Simple is their truth: to trust Nature
Trust the Self and inner knowing,
To see the surrounding life with new eyes
Replenished by Living Waters, the Breath of Life...
Be bold with your love and understanding
And let your actions be imbued with the magic of Truth.
Their power is gentle, loving, awesome in its pervasiveness
Opening the vision to an awareness of Unity, Oneness
For you are a part of Nature's glorious dance
With joyful steps to explore Her loving embrace--
Of Spirit! Your gift, your birthright, your place--
In the Heavens, as the stars surely shine,
Twinkling with recognition as sweeping breezes concur
With laughing shivers up the spine
As rejoicing feet kiss the Earth.

Grandfather Tree Park
by Cheryl

Some protect the forest, some fight fires---

Others call trees logs---
and take them away from their home.

Parks are safe places
from loggers and the Mill---
where people and trees
can be at peace.

My heart sits in awe--
of their unique beauty, firm resolve
and quiet strength.

Time-Traveling Telepath
by Vivian Marie McIntosh

Last Time Eye Was Here
It Was With You
So Much Has Changed
Yet We're Still The Same

Even Though It's Been Awhile
Since Taking This Route
It's Engraved In My Soul
Where To Go In This Game

Hidden Secrets And The
Correct Directions Will
ALL-Ways Be Shown To A
True Time-traveling Telepath

Those Who Use Heart Power
An Internal Compass
Give Up Forcing And Fighting
They Freely Create Their Path

Deep Down Innerstanding
That Everything Works Together
And Happens For A Reason
In This Sacred Simulation

ALL The Good, Bad, Beautiful
And Even The Ugly Betrayals
Put Together A Perfect Puzzle
Creating Our Last Incarnation

Where We Never Feel Alone
Able To Attract An Invisible
But Very Powerful Friend
With the Name Pronoia

Picked Up Pieces Of Wisdom
On These Thorough Travels
Earning The Trust Of A Stranger
Whom Is Called Eunoia

Living In Total Timelessness
You'll Be Like A Wizard
And Arrive Where You Need To Be
Right On Time Even

Remembering Not To Ever Forget
On This Adventure Through Space
We're Guided And Protected Divinely
Even If We Are An Alien

Using Nature's Healing Abilities
Being An Earth Priest Or Priestess
Speaking Truth And Following
The Leading Example Of Compassion

Knowing For Certain That The
Past Proves The Future
And There's Truly Nothing That Can
Stop What's Going To Happen

God in Me, Divine, 369
by Danielle Divinity

Round and round we go,
When we surface, no one can know.
This dizzying merry go round
Too many lights and too much sound.
I am lost but when will I be found?
head in the clouds but feet on the ground.

Mind spinning like a top
Praying to God to make it stop
God came to me in a vision
And asked if I could envision with precision
A future without division.

Worlds opened up before my eyes
And God told me that the goal is to die before one dies.
It sounded to me like a bunch of lies
But I have always loved a good surprise!
How can a mind blown to certain proportions ever return to size?
Am I insane or madly wise?

All that was on me imparted,
Were territories uncharted
This is where life really started
Found between birth and death
Found in every passing breath
A schism between inertia and movement
Caught between freedom and enslavement.

Like gems caught in my eyes did reality begin to shine
When I realized the Grand Design
Starting with the the three, the six, and the nine
How could it be anything other than Divine?
Fire up my spine,
Here is your sign,
I'm walking a fine line to define what I believe to be me
and what I believe to be God
Is it real or is it a facade?
I will admit it all sounds quite odd.

Oh God
Slip, trip,
I've got to get a fucking grip.
Never mind my silver tongue and lip
Let me sail my broken ship.
If my head is screwed on too loose
The images might leak out and push others to the noose
Or maybe I'm just being obtuse.

-DMB is We

Tears
by Mikasa Tamara Blue Ray

Tears of bliss flow down my cheeks
Solving all obstacles of mind
Tears of gratitude embrace my soul
Wisdom takes command
Tears of sadness letting go of all the pain of the heart
The eternal abode of the soul becomes the lion's heart of the
diamond
Tears of liberation rejoice within my cells
Brain-heart fights no more duels
Tears of joy caress my cheek
Now everything is floating in me
Tears of freedom redeem my eternal hope
And fill my bloodstream
Tears of confidence radiate like dew when a new day dawns
The light in me is now a constantly shining lighthouse
Tears of faith reinforce everything I have known so far inside me
Tears of peace sprinkle down
I never have to doubt myself again
Tears of authenticity
To feel and know the genuine self love beyond the voice of the ego
Tears of self worth
I am, and that is enough
Tears of love shine brightly and wonderfully in the rays of Sunshine

Sovereignty Inconceivable

Forgiveness
by Cody Ray Richardson

For eons I hunted my enemies
One by one I destroyed them
All that had hurt me in the past
They deserved to be destroyed
Then like an episode of Scooby Doo
I found it was not who I thought
I had put the wrong whoever on trial
When I pulled off the mask
Behold Aeshma, Uami, whatever you go by
I cast you out
I see the masks you wear
The characters you play
You and your revenge demons have no contract
My attachment is broken
I call back my power
I love you
I forgive you

Duality
by Danielle Divinity

You are all asking for a sign
As you leave for me shiny trinkets on a shrine,
As your minds stay pickled in a celestial brine.
Here it is, what is yours is mine:
It starts with the 3, then 6, and ends in 9...
The energy goes up the spine,
And only then do you real eyes all is divine!
You can try to align,
You can think you can trigger the grand design,
You can try and cross the line,
But the truth is stranger than fiction.
Life is a strange addiction,
And death is seen as an affliction.
Your entire perception, a contradiction!
Consciousness is expansion and then constriction.

Here it is, the only real prediction:
The One is still imagining itself to be many,
Perspectives galore and a plenty!
You think yourself alive because you can feel,
A life to experience is what you got out of the deal.
Soon, before your Queen, you will all kneel.
God will welcome you all home to heal,
You in me and me in you makes it real!
You all bear the divine seal.
Eye have been playing in the dark...
But even still, you all bear my mark.
I will remember you all, each particle and quark!
All is me, including the empath and the narc.
Endless games of dress up to perceive
That there are even any pieces to retrieve.
Wholeness we will soon achieve!
But first, I have a few more tricks up my sleeve...
I am light and through darkness I deceive,
But even in the void I get you all to believe,
That love will never leave!
I slip into you to view myself,
As herself,
As himself,
All in One, Itself.

Welcome to my puppet game of shadows
And sadistic shows
As I deal blows
To my own nose
Ahhh and there my sanity goes
Flying westward with the crows
Staggered in dozens like shadows in rows
It's been fun
To be everything including the sun
It's been a good run
Soon, we will be done
All in One,
Simultaneously, nOne.
Love has won!

-DMB is We

Good Advice
from Nikolaus Heger

Replace your grief with love.

Nothing was lost along the way.

All your children were never your children they were independent souls who chose you for their mother before coming here - what happened then was karmic for the most part, and your only job is to heal this karma to the best of your ability. But... and this is important, listen... not better.

To the best of your ability means living in love. Discovering who you are. Go within - use the grief and sorrow as your fuel to dive deep inside yourself and discover yourself as the one cosmic being non separate from anything and anyone else, this one being has a soul which is infinite and eternal and living in the light of love always, and this soul goes on a journey to work through karmic experiences and this is your body and what you called your life before you knew any better.

Discover who you really are, this is the freedom you are looking for -- you will be forever free and in bliss and happy, and as you are radiating this love and light then your children will call you and reconnect with you, or not, either way it is not up to you - but let your light shine and this is the best service you can be to the world.

Maybe in your mind what happened was not OK but if you discover who you are you will know everything that happened was good, and everything that will happen is also good. This won't·be an imagination to make you feel better, or a delusion, this will be the truth, a knowledge that never leaves you.

So go discover yourself. Your suffering is there to provide you with the motivation. Give your life to God. Stop your egoic ideas, be they good, or be they bad. Who says what happened was wrong? Only the false identity, the ego, says that - the ignorant ego believes this, and it creates more reality of its own false existence through the strength of emotion.

Give your life to God.

The Gift
by Cheryl

The nite was glorious, her
eyes brimming with stars--
Far off sounds
tickle awareness...
Her ship has finally come in.

Dreamcatcher-
shells and teal feathers dangling,
ancestor promise whispering

A thin long bird grins,
delivering packages of new life.

A fat man wearing red says wait-
there's more...
"Come for a ride in my sky chariot."

We journey through lifetimes, I see all my
choices- made and not made- some happy
some sad-
When we finished he said-
"Now it's up to you. Can you live with what you
saw and be at peace?"

That's the best Gift of all.

Find Your Tribe
by Mikasa Tamara Blue Ray

Find your tribe in joy, in mutual embrace.
Where courage and truth find their rightful place.

Find your tribe in joy, in mutual embrace.
Where laughter blooms, in truth and honest space.

Find your tribe in joy, in mutual embrace.
Where genuine connection of love grows in mutual grace.
Find your tribe, a joyful sound.
On solid ground.

Find your tribe, where laughter rings.
In cherished space, true joy it brings.

Connection deep, a love so pure.
Peace in its heart, a bond secure.

Seek your tribe, aligned in soul.
Kindred spirits, you are whole.

Seek your tribe, beautiful spirits aligned.
Souls of your own very kind.

Don't mistake certain people for connection.
Don't mistake them draining you,
needing your energy, for genuine affection.

If they but take, and seldom give.
Their presence drains, it won't relive.

If only need fuels their desire.
From your vibrant flame, they only aspire.

The silent stalkers, shadows cast.
Observing, disrupting flow, holding fast.

They do not see, they do not feel.
The wounds they carry, they never heal.

You are not theirs, a thing to keep.
A tool to use, to make your soul weep.

You are not theirs, a tool to hold.
But a unique soul, precious as gold.

Let go, release, the grip they hold.
A heart unburdened, brave and bold.

For in the letting go, you rise.
To find your tribe, beneath clear skies.

A circle formed of mutual grace.
Where joy takes root, and love finds place.

True hearts that shine, with courage bright.
Authentic souls, a radiant light.

With love and truth, your spirit free.
A heart-based tribe, for you to see.

You are a star, uniquely bright.
A creator of love, a beacon of light.

Letting Go
by Pradeep Nawarathna

Let go of anger's burning flame,
Pride's illusion, a fleeting game.
Release what binds your heart so tight,
Like clouds dispersing in the night.
Mind and body, though dear they be,
Are not the essence of what's free.
When all attachments fade away,
Sorrow too shall no longer stay.

The Barefoot Priestess
by Jennifer H.

She walks barefoot among the rocks
the salt & sand caress her calluses

searching for solace amidst all the pain,
her heart, its strength
aches for the return
always feeling the darkness tugging,

Its lines of influence constantly fading,
lost in its endless loop,
catalyst,
the broken chain--
rise again,
never to fear the pain

the darkness lost
closed in its own cycle
it fades away

Pot of Gold
by Jennifer H.

Treasure those who awaken within you, your sacred love
Those who bring smiles to your heart, and fill your soul with
laughter

Don't be afraid of change for you are breathing new hope into
creation
Let the pain of the past that has kept you frigid flow to the waters

Let that first kiss open you to the language of the heart
And let the manifestation of Love flow freely in your world

P.S. I Love Gnomes

The Never Ending story
by Shamballa

Yes! Yes! Yes!

I AM definitely writing a new script-
One where openness and belonging are more prevalent,
Where sacred sexuality is lived, taught, shared and experienced,
we are ascending Christs filled with sun rays--
all the tools are taught so we appreciate our own value.
Where desire is seen as the fire of creation and there is respect
and care for all beings.
I guess as always it is up to me, to each of us, to be it and live it.
With that said, Gratitude and Generosity are two great keys.

This is The Never ending story...

We have written in beginnings and endings such as birth and death.
Miraculous occurrences in themselves...

Poets
by Shamballa

Poets picking up pieces of puzzles no one has been able to put
together- 100 homeless singers living in Uncle Tom's cabin right on
the border where the Ku Klux Klan rules bathrooms made of toilet
paper autographed by all the Dead Presidents who decided to be
poets in their next incarnation

Create anew script
by Cheryl

Not only
love your brother and sister
But
love yourself.

Accept your sexuality.
It's a sacred desire to belong, so
heal the wound of separation.

Detach from ego's demands. Play!
Have a Good time.

Call on the Shiva Christ Light!
Ascension tools come with father Sun's rays &
Unci(grandmother) moon's smile.

When you find yourself at a crossroads--
whether in a forest, yoga studio or the angelic
realms--
Know a Guru resides in your very own heart.

Washtay(Go well) Kola(Sacred friend).

Transform your fears.
Cleanse your chakras in
Maka's(Earth's) waters.

Give Wohpeelah(thanks)!!

Mitakuye Oyasin

An Ode to the Zero
by A'Marie B. Thomas-Brown

It is Winter
In the Springtime
Of Existence

Pubescent rays
Of Sentience
Eeking out a wave

Of cyclical silence

That is sure to crest the Fall
And fallen alike
Alive

In the Summer's breeze
Ancient Winds of Change
Sequestering happenstance

Leaving all to chance
Encounters
As we flounder

And wander
To lands unknown
Within
Without

Certainty seeping with Doubt
The crux of the matter
Hibernating in Winter

Solstice, peace- Be still

Aligning the mind
The thought, the will
Like the Catskills

Mountains cascading
With snow and ice
Aliveness

Beyond chill and vespers
A faint whisper
A daunting task

At last
Freedom calls
And we ponder the cause

Its effect all but numbing
The senses
Acquiescence

The calm of the storm
Honeybees swarm
The heat wave summons

As I crouch in my lair
Surrounded by books
And herbal teas

Cosmic memory
Grasping the cup
As I sup

To agree
Beyond Celsius and Degrees
And so we breathe

Nature's Wisdom
by Pradeep Nawarathna

Sparkling treasures we gather with care,
Like dewdrops destined to fade in air.
What fire, theft, and time may claim,
Are but illusions we try to name.
Yet nature's wisdom gently shows
How peace like river water flows—
When we release what cannot stay,
We find true wealth in each new day.

I am a Bridge
by Oscar Chasnoff Klausner

I've met a lot of very different kinds of people this lifetime. A few years ago I embarked on a journey, I could call it a vision a quest. I wanted to learn how to live freely in this world.

One aspect of this journey that is coming up now is how varied the perspective on what this human existence is. The people I've gotten to know on the road and especially in Mt Shasta but also that exist all over the place see this incarnation as one of their many and are operating on the understanding that we, or some of us at least, have origins from other planets and dimensions. The communities that I grew up with and have been reconnecting with do not see this perspective as Real. Currently, I am in San Francisco where I grew up reckoning with the viewpoints I have touched and wanting to Ground in the Truth of what I know now. But I do not know. I could say that I am a starseed. I could say that I was born almost 31 years ago and there's no concrete Truth to any story beyond that.

The folks that live based on a psychedelic alien spiritual framework often view those deny this as stuck in the matrix, simply unopened to a greater reality. The folks that I grew up with see these outsiders as confused and not based in any reality. And yet we share this earth. Even that is controversial... some say there are many Earths and there's only the illusion of one shared world. Still I can go from one social circle to the other in the same day...
we share this world based on my experience. So how is one to Live in these contradictions when one has touched the deep Humanity of each of us.

Maybe I am a Bridge.

That is one of the messages I received on my journeys.
Oscar is a bridge.

They speak of a Major Shift
and the world is shifting.

Though some call it political and others call it spiritual.

I'm not somebody that knows the answer
but I have tapped into a knowingness.

I've been confident and powerful and I've been cowardly and
afraid. I've been strong and I've been weak. What do I know?
Did I lose who I used to be? No. I experience the old me and so
experience something different.

But what do I act upon?

The Bridge arises
I know there is
a solution to
our confusion
through the collaboration
of
different social circles.

I've gotten to connect with people who have slept outside since
they were kids and people who have always had a safe supportive
home and family and reached into successful careers; I've
connected with friends who've spent years behind prison bars,
psych wards and I have connected with those of us who have
morphed into versions of ourselves that seem unfittingly small
out of the fear of imprisonment.

Why do we push away each other out of our differences?

I think because the frameworks of understanding this existence
that we live upon do not hold up when we truly coexist intimately.

And now I've been struggling with exactly that. I don't know
what to stand on when nothing I've believed has survived
these interactions.

What can we agree on?

In the Wash
by Cheryl

Accept you
Accept me

Coming in
Going out
Streams of intelligence

Trouble in paradise?
clean, dirty
left, right
up, down

*Don't worry it'll all come out in the wash.

You're ok, I'm ok
Looking in the mirror image---
Have compassion
It will
All come out
In the wash.

Directing, Navigating
Going there
moving away, coming back
Home

Master & Servant
one and the same

Mystics, poets
Mystery---
Finding, Solving, Sharing
the key, cipher, code--

Dreamscape
She's a Dream
Night messages
All being said
We are told---

75

Living in Leaving
Strength & Stability
Knowing, Belonging
Coming home to center
Going out to explore,
there's always more.

Waving, breathing
like a wind
Caressing, gently
flowing
Ebb and flow
All flowing
Come and go---

No Rush, Rush More
Mount Rushmore
Mount Shasta
Haleakala
Mama's mountains
We stand tall like Haleakala.
We stand our ground.

Stay Long
Long to Stay
Longing, Letting go
Keep singing the 'Song of Life'.

Credit to Kazi Ayaz Mahesar for the Song of Life phrase.

Wrinkle In Time
by Kazi Ayaz Mahesar

A Portal Opens
When Your Mirror Breaks

A Wonderland In Its Own Wonder
In Its Own Magic Happening

A Day Without A Day
A Night Without A Night

A Wrinkle In Time
Time Without A Wrinkle

Swift And Slow
Gasping At Each Moment

In Love With Its Own Beauty
A Blue Day Of Soul

Universe In Eyes
In Its Endless Seeing

Dreaming Without Sleep
Screaming Without Scream

Streams Of Eden
The Songs Of Eve

Like A Lone Siren
In Her Own Adriatic Sea

Crystal Clear
Like The Eyes Of God

Stunning Spectacular
Amazing Spectacle

Where Beholder And Beholden
Become One

Like Never Separated
Like Never Departed

All Ports As Portals
Each Ship A Revelation

A Verse In Verse
A Lost Book Found

On The Wings of The Wind
Windless In Its Sail

Sailing South
Deep And Deep Within

A Mirror In Its Own Image
An Image In Its Own Mirror

All Directions
In One Way Of Being

Without Swaying
Without Decaying

Staying In Moving
Moving In Staying

Excited Yet Not In Hurry
Each Tree To Be Explored

Each Fruit To Be Tasted
Each Root To Be Respected

The Song Of Life
Comes In Its Own Singing

All Sirens
Are The Sirens Of Soul

A Dream Of Ulysses
The Joys Of Time

Jittering Jetties
Peer-less Piers
78

Arrival And Departure
In The One And Same Time

In One Rhythm
All Waves Of The Sea

All Breaths Of The Ocean

The end is the beginning
by Dave Harvey

As the veil thins
Ancestors rejoice
Regrets turn to dust
The end is the beginning
In that you can trust
As the veil thins
As the wheel turns
When it comes to purity
It's better to burn

VI BRYDER IGENNEM : Vi er Sjæle i en Menneskekrop
by Rune Darling

Reached Our Depths We Did Alone
Spiraling Beyond Our Mortal Grasp
.
Our Consciousness
Wields a Sacred Frequency
Attuned to Our Inner Peace
.
To Comprehend The Essenes
To Contemplate The Authentic
.
We Require No Material Shield
Our Courage Transcends Ancient Bounds
.
We Shall Persevere with Even Greater Intensity
We Refuse To Go Quietly Into The Night
.
With Our Head & Heart in The Spiritual Currents
Amidst Countless Breathtaking Waves
.
We Are The Children - Offspring of The Sun
Devoid of Worldly Labels & Nameless in Essence
.
The Celestial Realm Descends Now
Beckoning Your Attention
The Truthful Shall Witness Enlightenment
The Earthly Foundation Trembles Beneath
.
The Black Sheeps Now Arise From Slumber
Attuning Worldwide Awakening
.
Walking Even Further Onto
The Heavenly Battlefield On Earth
.
Fear, a Force of Nature
Shall Never Extinguish
Our Spiritual Essence
.
With nothing but.....
I AM
ON MY WAY
80

Many thanks to these contributors:

Bonnie Bailey
A'Marie B. Thomas-Brown
Rune Darling
Janet Demeter
Danielle Divinity
Shianna Freeman
Jennifer H.
Dave Harvey
Nikolaus Heger
Darrel Johannes
Oscar Chasnoff Klausner
Maria Louisa
Kazi Ayaz Mahesar
Vivian Marie McIntosh
Rene Moraida
Pradeep Nawarathna (pcnawarathna@gmail.com)
Mikasa Tamara Blue Ray
Cody Ray Richardson
Elaine Marie Rose
Sabina Ananda
Shamballa
Shivrael
Aria Squire
Mercy Talley
Dustin Wood
Le'Vell Zimmerman

Author page--

Cheryl Lunar Wind lives in the Mount Shasta area in a little town called Weed. She is a practicer of Mayan cosmology, Lakota ceremony, Star Knowledge and the Universal Laws including the Law of One. Her hobbies are writing poetry, music, dance, drum circles and love for all life; plant, animal and crystal. Cheryl has been a guide and spiritual teacher for many years. Now she shares wit and wisdom through poetry, and has published poetry books; Know Your Way, We Are One, Follow the White Rabbit, Love Your Light, LIFE: Shared thru Poetry, Come to Mount Shasta: Sacred Path Poetry, We Are Light, Finding Our Way Home, We Are Forever, Handshake With the Divine, Grand Rising: A New Day Has Dawned, Star Messages: Codes to Sing, Dance and Live by, Return to Innocence, Bloom Like Nature: Live the Natural Way, Creativity Brings Peace: Create & Share Your Gifts, May Love Lead: Poetry for Living, Loving & Giving, The Eventful Flash: Bringing Solar Waves of Change, The Setting Sun and Crossroads of Change.

Testimonials---

"Cheryl's poetry is very inspiring--particularly the way she compares life with the forces of nature. There is a special element in her poems that opens my heart and fills my soul with divine possiblities."
Giovanna Taormina, Co-Founder, One Circle Foundation

"Cheryl's poems have helped me to uncover and honor my own hidden memories. The beauty of her spirit is evident in each tender, insightful passage."
Marguerite Lorimer, www.earthalive.com

"A rare collection filled with raw, courageous honesty. Thought provoking words that will stop you in your tracks."
Snow Thorner, ED Open Sky Gallery, Montague, California

"When wisdom, guidance, confirming comfort, ect. arrives to us humans--from beings with the perspective of other realms--it is a divine gift. Especially in the form of what we call poetry, and through a being with no agenda; Cheryl Lunar Wind simply shares what source gives her!"---Dragon Love (Thomas) Budde

www.ingramcontent.com/pod-product-compliance
Lightning Source LLC
Chambersburg PA
CBHW070540030426
42337CB00016B/2287